MANAGING TEAM DEVELOPMENT

A short guide for teams and team managers

Edited by Gwen Rosen

Managing Team Development
A short guide for teams and team managers

Published 1999
by the National Institute for Social Work
5 Tavistock Place, London WC1H 9SN
www.nisw.org.uk
email info@nisw.org.uk

© National Institute for Social Work

All rights reserved. No part of this publication may be reproduced or transmitted in any form or by any means, electronic, mechanical, photocopying, recording or otherwise, or stored in any retrieval system of any nature, without prior permission of the publisher.

ISBN 1 899942 31 9

Cover designed by Pat Kahn

Printed by Meridian Print Centre Ltd, Derby

Contents

Contributors		iv
Introduction		v
Section 1:	Defining the Team	1
Section 2:	Establishing the Team and its work	6
Section 3:	Using the Team's Knowledge, Skills and Experience	9
Section 4:	Managing Change and Innovation	11
Section 5:	Service Development and Innovation	18
Section 6:	Teamload Management	21
Section 7:	Knowledge Based Practice	24
Useful References		26

Contributors

John Brown:		Newcastle Social Services Department

Trish Kearney:	National Institute for Social Work

Gwen Rosen:		National Institute for Social Work

Gerry Smale:		National Institute for Social Work

Many thanks to all the team managers who generously contributed to this booklet, and in particular Sylvia Agaas, Caroline Babb, Mary Hirst, Vanessa Price, Phil Sawbidge and Fiona Wallace.

Introduction

'We have so much work to do, the last thing we need is an invitation to start thinking about what we do!'

The Director of The Children's Society in his foreword to *Systems Thinking for Harassed Managers*

About the guide and how to use it

This booklet has been written to enable team managers to develop the practice of the team. It is divided into sections which all interrelate but each section can be used alone. The aim of this booklet is to act as a trigger or starter for team discussions about examining and developing standards of practice.

The areas covered in the booklet have been identified as important by teams in a variety of social work and social care settings. The exercises outlined have been tried and tested, mainly during work on the National Institute for Social Work (NISW) project 'Management of Practice Expertise.'

Each section of the booklet contains:

- a summary of the main issues for discussion with the team
- some exercises which help to illustrate the area under discussion.

The work outlined is not intended to replace the more traditional individual supervision that social workers are used to, but is a complementary activity focusing on the collective work of team members.

This booklet is an invitation to think about social work practice. It is our experience that discussions about practice issues have become a rarity for busy social work teams. However, they are necessary. Do not hurry through team discussions or any of the exercises you may decide to carry out.

Section 1
Defining the team

Here we present some issues and questions for discussion with team members. Sections 1 and 2 should help teams:

- outline team autonomy
- establish team boundaries
- define team tasks.

The main characteristics of a team are:

- three or more people
- an agreed structure
- a team identity and shared tasks.

Almost all social workers are located in teams. This can be an administrative device only. Examine who is **really** in the team or are there teams within teams?

How are the 'support' members of the team (administrators for example) integral to the work of the team? Do they feel that they are the last to hear about things? Are they a team within a team?

What is a realistic size for team working? Between 6 to 11 members is usually considered appropriate but this can vary enormously. Communication between team members is crucial. Teams that are big (over 15 members) rarely meet together and if they are located in different venues will find communication and a sharing of a common and agreed task difficult.

How much autonomy teams have depends on the 'culture' of the organisation they work in. Teams often have a great deal of autonomy and capacity to decide on their task. Within the parameters of the organisation's aims, team managers and their team members are in the best position to make judgements about their work – what can and cannot be done and how to be responsive to the needs of the particular area or client group they serve. However, this means that teams need to have good intelligence about their locality or their client group and their needs.

The team needs to know the stated aims and plans of the organisation. The Community Care Plan, Children's Plan and any departmental or organisational business plan, give written guidance to teams on the parameters or 'skeleton' on which to base their own team aims and plans. It is the experience of most teams that these plans allow discretion for individual teams to exemplify their purpose and task, although the amount of discretion can vary considerably between local authorities.

The limits of this discretion are not always tested out by team managers and their knowledge can be based on myth rather than actual limitations. There also may be some ambivalence by manager and team members about testing out the discretionary boundaries. Are you clear as a team and team manager about the boundaries around you when making decisions about your work? Is it clearly stated in your organisation or is there a lot of custom and practice behaviour? What happens if you overstep your decision making boundary? How would you know when you have overstepped?

Defining the task of the team is a dynamic process which has to be restated from time to time. Changes in locality or neighbourhood characteristics, changes in law, changes in political policy and changes in social work and organisational practice, all require the team to reassess its purpose and function. To obtain a degree of consensus for all team members on the purpose and function of the team can take time. However, failure to address this issue can lead to poor practice and confusion for both staff and service users.

Team leadership is important but not all tasks have to be led by the team manager. To have credibility with a team, the team manager should be able to take on most of the team's tasks even if she or he cannot carry them out with the same degree of expertise as another team member. However, the manager's ability to carry out most team tasks may become less possible as social work practice moves increasingly towards specialisation. The manager who can only manage others and is without practice expertise is at a disadvantage in social work.

The team manager needs to delegate, not to suit him or herself but for the most effective working of the team. Delegation needs to be made explicit and communicated clearly.

To help establish the purpose of the team use the following exercises.

Exercise 1

Check whether there is any written material already in place which describes the purpose and tasks of the team. This can be a useful starting point even if it is out of date.

Exercise 2

Use the grid on page 4 to map out the activities of the team. The dimensions of this grid are not alternatives, and for most service users, social work activities will cover a range of activities.

4 • Managing team development

Each team member can do this for his or her work, or the exercise can be done by the team for the team. Teams have found this grid a useful outline for establishing a 'picture' of their work.

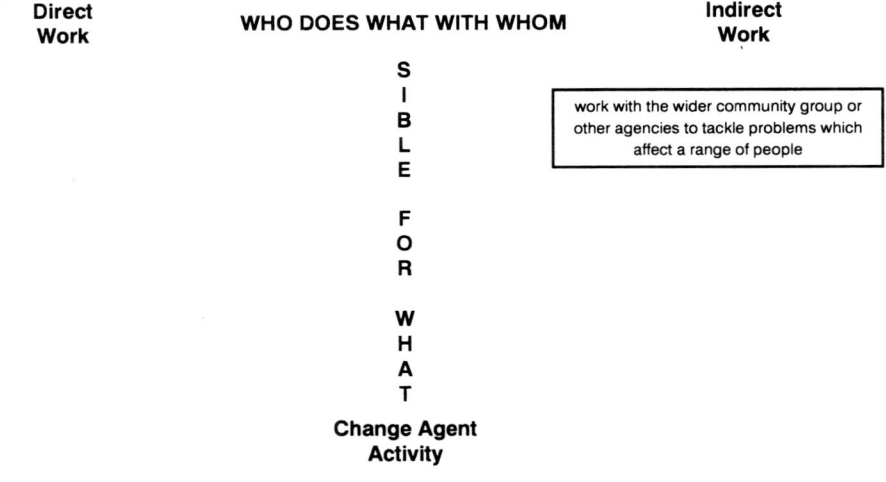

This grid is from Smale G. and Tuson G. with Biehal, N. and Marsh, P. (1993) *Empowerment, Assessment, Care Management and the Skilled Worker*. London:HMSO p. 33–34

Exercise 3

Ask each team member to imagine they are meeting an interested and friendly colleague at a conference and are asked to describe the purpose of their team. Ask team members to relate what they would say to the person sitting next to them (their neighbour) in the team meeting. Ask the 'neighbour' to write it down and then put responses up on a flip chart.

This can be a very revealing exercise. It can also lead to a discussion as to why there may be certain blocks to actually carrying out the team's function or how realistic the agreed purpose of the team is.

Section 2
Establishing the team and its work

The organisation has placed your team on its family tree. This is likely to be a one dimensional, administrative map, showing reporting, communication and possibly budgeting lines. This map probably determines the pattern of your team meetings: the forum for collective activity. Despite the many structural reorganisations your department is likely to have undergone in recent years, the appearance of this map has probably changed very little. It may reflect certain assumptions:

- that teams are small in number
- that they are geographically close
- that they cover one main task for their organisation and are therefore made up of people doing interchangeable jobs.

Organisations worry constantly about time spent in meetings. Individuals echo this when they complain that team meetings deal only with top-down information distribution. Team managers are often faced with running a meeting with an overlong agenda for a large group of disparate workers.

Exercise 4

These are questions for the whole team to consider. Give yourselves one and a half hours.

- Do the assumptions of the administrative map adequately describe your team?
- How many people are in the team as a whole? If more than 12, the team is probably struggling with too many cross-references to function effectively as the main channel for development.
- How geographically spread are they?
- How many teams within the team can you identify? Where does allegiance and sense of membership lie for the individual?
- How many people in the team find themselves in more than one of these groupings?
- Are there outside teams that team members also belong to: for example, a multidisciplinary mental health team or an administrative team in the building?
- How many of these groupings are about common tasks and skills, rather than organisational titles: eg. initial assessment, therapeutic change, risk management?

Draw a map that displays these characteristics.

- What new groupings does the map show?

Case example

A front line children's team consists of 18 people based on the same site. The team considers itself to have high morale, commitment to developing best practice, good working relationships with each other and a well thought of team manager. They meet regularly as a whole team every two weeks. They find this frustrating: they compete for the floor in the time available; the team manager finds such a large group difficult to lead cohesively. Workers' practice concerns fight for attention and they describe attending the meeting as either boring when their own interests are not addressed or are frustrated at the lack of time when they are.

As a result of carrying out Exercise 4, the team in the example has reconsidered how to run its team meeting. The large group meets much less frequently, with an agenda of standing items defined by them. They have set up a number of practice development groups that span the various job titles and that are focused on the collective tasks they have defined. Some of the artificial barriers between workers have disappeared: duty workers and direct workers with children have identified their common expertise and development interests; administrators no longer have to choose between job title solidarity (their membership of a wider administrators group) and their contribution to the primary tasks of the service (working as a member of the duty team).

The team has articulated some of the barriers to change they had feared, by being explicit about their particular skills and expertise, not least the worry that everyone will be expected to do everything. They have been able to move past their collective worry about making their own interests prominent at the expense of those of their colleagues. The team manager has the coordinating and monitoring role over these new activities, making better use of her contribution to a strategic overview and leadership.

Section 3
Using the team's knowledge, skills and experience

Section 3 should help you to:

- learn from the team's collective experience, knowledge and skills
- establish current best practice in the team
- support a collective approach to the work of the team
- define the development needs of the team.

Traditionally social workers learn their craft as individuals. Supervision is usually on a one to one basis, and training courses that remove individuals from their work setting invariably miss out on collective benefits to the team. Learning is often regarded as knowledge from outside imparted in a variety of ways to the individual. Opportunities for workbased learning have redressed this balance but can still default into this mode when training materials repeat 'empty vessels to be filled' notions of learning. Paradoxically the expertise available to the team lies within their own experiences at work and with the experts in the problems they are presented with, namely the families and communities that come to them for help. The following exercise presumes that:

- There are no easy answers: if there were, your clients would not need you.

- Struggling with intractable and complex situations does not mean that you are doing your job badly.
- By focusing on the difficulties that workers experience in isolation, the team can think about the collective skills and knowledge they can draw on for the problems they are asked to deal with.
- You are of most use to your clients as a problem solver, not a solution provider, although providing services may be a part of what you do.

As leader of this exercise you may wish to discuss these presumptions with the team as a basis for sharing practice.

Exercise 5

Choose a practice issue that you want to apply your collective wisdom to: in other words, something that a number of you find difficult or intractable. The material for discussion is provided by the direct work undertaken by individual team members. Both the team manager and team members need to help the worker presenting material feel 'safe', especially if this is a new experience for them. However, it should also be remembered that presenting and discussing your work is part of any professional practice. The presentation will describe the initial referral, the worker's aims, actions and decisions taken and the difficulties they currently experience with the work.

Next, the team uses this information to consider:

- Who is involved: the social and the professional networks.
- The different perspectives of these people, including their concerns. How would a worker know? Has the worker spoken to each individual involved?

Section 3 Using the team's knowledge, skills and experience • 11

- What the service user or family wants and why, and how would a worker know this?
- The worker's role: is the worker to be a solution provider or a problem solver? A problem solver is someone from outside the immediate situation with a fresh point of view.
- What do the participants think the worker's role is? What has the worker told them? What should the worker tell them?
- The social situation that has led to the referral and how a worker could give this outsider view to the people involved. How can a worker acknowledge the feelings of the individuals involved and the part feelings play in its problem?
- What does the team know about working with this type of referral? How can they use this knowledge and experience to help them in this case?

Once you have looked together at the case(s):

- What kind of conversations does the worker need to have to undertake an assessment of need?
- What information and knowledge will help the individual worker?
- What information does the worker need to give to the participants?
- How might you 'capture' the knowledge you have produced from your collective experience?
- Have you identified any gaps in the team's skills that could be strengthened either by team members' contributions or from outsiders?
- If knowledge could be strengthened by people from outside the team, what are the routes available in your

organisation for obtaining this expertise? Inviting appropriate staff from other teams or organisations to present their work at your team meeting can be useful, stimulating and will increase the team's knowledge base.

This exercise is essentially a group supervision session. It does not replace the need for individual staff supervision and should not be viewed as an alternative to individual supervision.

Section 4
Managing change and innovation

All staff in social services and social care have change, to a greater or lesser degree, as part of their task. A common oversimplification is to assume that managers initiate, lead or direct staff into change. It is more likely that staff are leaders of some change, supporters of some, and feel victims and opponents of other change.

No approach to managing change can guarantee that you will achieve the desired outcomes. You will not be in control of all the variables that effect change. However, you can increase your chances of success by addressing certain key issues and questions.

Exercise 6

Map all the people involved in the proposed changes.

The first step in the process of managing change is to draw up a map of **all** the people involved in the path of changing practice. This enables you to begin to identify the significant people, reflect on their attitudes to the application of the particular targeted changes and to recognise that there are more people involved than initially anticipated.

Mapping is central to identifying who has to do what and with whom. It is possible to draw up a list of critical activities, or negotiations, based on recognising key people, where they 'stand' on the innovation, what they need to be doing for the innovation to be implemented, what relationships need to change and so on.

Use the map to describe:

- the innovation that you want to introduce
- the problem that it addresses
- the people involved in the status quo that it replaces.

Maps should include all people involved or affected by the change. Try to name names wherever possible.

Following the mapping exercise, there are a number of key questions to ask when initiating change with a team. As a team manager you may want to regard the following questions as a framework for team discussions, in effect, a series of conversational exercises.

The questions will help both the team and the manager identify crucial areas for discussion:

- What is the problem?

It is useful to recognise that all changes are composed of a **series** of innovations. It is also helpful to be clear why change is taking place – or put another way – what problem is being addressed or resolved by the proposed changes.

It is crucial for people to understand why change is taking place – although different people will have different reasons. Throughout the change process you will need to keep asking a number of other questions as a team. These include:

- For whom is the status quo a problem?
- Who wants change and for what reasons?
- How do the service users or customers see the problem?

Often resistance is the natural reaction of people to change. Much so called resistance to change can be understood as a negative response to the change agents themselves about:

- their definition of the problem
- their chosen solution
- the way they are managing change.

Further key questions to discuss as a team are:

- How does the innovation fulfil the organisation's mission and contribute to its major aims?
- How does it fit with the objectives of good practice?
- How does it match service users' perceptions of what they want and need?

Revisit your map of change and address the following questions:

- What changes and what **stays the same**? This is a crucial question.
- Who needs to make it happen and take action for change?
- Who has to let it happen and who has to keep out of the way?
- Is it a change **within** the rules or a change **in** the rules?

A useful way of understanding change within or in the rules is to see it as 'first order' or 'second order' change in relationships between people.

A first order change is a change **within** the rules of a given system, **within** the existing pattern of relationships, between people even where tasks may change significantly. First order change takes place without change in the existing role relationships between people. Second order change, on the other hand, occurs when there is a change **in** the rules, a change **in** the nature of the system, when the rules and the boundaries of a system of relationships change.

Managers initiating second order change have to alter what they do **when they are an integral part of the relationship being affected by change**. First order changes involve renegotiating tasks and methods. Second order changes involve renegotiating tasks, methods and roles **and relationships**.

Responses to change

- From whom are you getting positive responses?
- From whom are you getting negative responses?
- Who is reacting positively or negatively to the innovation itself?
- Who is reacting positively or negatively to the way that the innovation is being introduced?
- Does the innovation still address the problems it is supposed to? What consequences does the innovation have beyond those intended?

People's reaction to change will depend on at least three major interrelated dimensions:

- Firstly, are they active or passive?

  'To have the rug pulled from under you is a very different experience from coming to a decision to reject the old flooring and choose a new carpet, or to move to another room.'

  'Those who only care if they have their hands on the rug and want to get the job done in the quickest possible way

can expect to meet with great opposition, and take a long time to get through, or over it.'

- Secondly, does the innovation produce a change of identity?
- Thirdly, what do key people win or lose?

People's so-called resistance is often caused by their anticipated loss of identity through change. These losses are often compounded and sometimes even caused by the way change is mismanaged rather than as a response to the innovation itself.

These considerations lead to our next and final questions:

- What meaning does the status quo and the innovation or change have for all the key people involved?
- For whom does the innovation change the purpose of the task?
- How does the innovation change the motivation of significant people?
- Who will experience a change in status or image of themselves?
- What symbolic significance is attached to the status quo by key players?

This section on managing change is a brief introduction. For further reading about this complex, lengthy and often difficult task, consult Smale, G. (1996) *Mapping Change and Innovation*. London: HMSO.

Section 5
Service development and innovation

Being a member of a team which is innovative in its practice and which is at the cutting edge of service delivery is invigorating and empowering for its members and brings increased benefits for its service users. Team members report enormous satisfaction levels when they are members of a team within which they are allowed and encouraged to experiment, innovate, and learn through their reflective practice.

Service development begins with an 'inside-the-team' analysis and assessment of performance which is based on **locally** owned and accepted data about problems in the delivery of the team's services. Data which demonstrates that practice is less than ideal can be introduced alongside a team agreement to improve and learn more creative and more effective ways of delivering practice. The drive to improve practice is more favourably received when it emerges from 'within team' debates and 'within team' discussions, rather than being an expectation set, or an instruction given, from outside the team.

However, the encouragement of senior managers, or at least their acceptance of service development being initiated and carried out by teams, is important. Service development entails accepting that there is no 'steady state' or homeostasis. Constant contextual shifts and service development is normal.

Development and continuous learning about new practice is promoted by asking questions such as:

- Why are we still doing this?
- Why does it still have to be done this way?

These discussions need to take place initially with team members but the team manager will also have to 'sell' and promote the changes with others outside his or her team. Raising such questions and issues also entails having team leaders who are willing to relinquish past practices while embracing the future in the pursuit of practice improvements.

Integral to any service development or practice change are evaluation and monitoring measures. Again, these need to be discussed and initially developed with the team but there may be advice and guidance for the team from support staff who specialise in service evaluation measures or from universities.

The manager with accountability responsibilities, but who is also a service developer, has a more empowering relationship with the new practice developers if she works in partnership with them. It is usually the new practice developers who rapidly progress from early experimentation to practice expertise. Supervisors therefore need to display humility and willingness to admit their limitations but accept accountability for the results of their attempts at encouraging their practitioners to be innovative, evaluative and experimental.

Exercise 7

In a team meeting, group supervision or a quality improvement session (or in one to one supervision), ask the following questions:

- Why are we still doing this?
- Why does it still have to be done this way?
- Does it still work? Is there a better way of doing it?
- Should we be doing it at all?

Also explore:

- What would happen if we pursued several of these options? What would this look like in practice?

Your team will be helped in this exercise if you can gather information about the team's performance that is both subjective and objective (qualitative and quantitative).

Exercise 8

Consider, if you can, all the changes you and your team want to make. This makes the principles of service development more explicit.

Then explore the following questions about developing services:

- What are the staff and service user comments about what's wrong at present?
- What would you change in your service if you were a service user?
- What does local data tell you about your services and service problems?

Points to bear in mind when developing services:

- Promote continuous service effectiveness, evaluation and assessment and be flexible about what works with whom.
- Constantly strive for service improvements. Make space for service development and continue to try to find additional resources – never accept 'It can't be done!'
- Support front line staff in shaping the team's future direction – team leaders cannot do it alone.
- Create and promote independent thinking within your team – disagreement with your team leader does not mean disloyalty.
- Promote continuous training and personal development in line with continuously revised team objectives.

Section 6
Teamload management

This section looks at teamload management. This differs from caseload and workload management. Caseload management concentrates on the allocated cases of an individual worker. It may measure risk presented and complexity but could be a straightforward listing of allocated cases. Workload management is more likely to measure actual time spent and so will consider a number of activities beyond the caseload, for example travelling time and administration.

Both caseload and workload systems focus on the work of an individual and can be used to ensure equity of effort across a team. They help individual professional development by offering a framework in which to review the fit between experience and the development of skills. They are also often aggregated across administrative divisions of a department and provide information for senior management.

Teamload management differs in its focus as it considers **the total work of any team**. It differs in its purpose from caseload and workload systems in that initially it is information collected and used **within** the team and **by** the team, although the picture of practice it presents may usefully be applied to the department as a whole. All teams need to know about the referral rate, the range and quality of work undertaken by the whole team and team outputs.

To allocate and assess the volume of work, a team needs to have a teamload system. It needs to include all the work of the team as identified in such exercises as the mapping exercise described in Section 1.

The team will need to agree some definitions or ensure it is using departmental definitions, if they already exist. For example, is the work with a family regarded as one case, or a series of cases, possibly with different social workers involved? Any teamload system needs to be simple and easy to administer and applicable to the work setting of the team. Although teamload is primarily the responsibility of the team manager, all team members should be able to access the system and the system needs to be open and transparent to scrutiny.

Teamload systems are best utilised when they are owned by all team members, are not the brain child of the team manager and are an accepted part of organisational practice. This means that team members have been involved in the design or adaptation of the system which suits their needs and their work setting. Social services organisations already collect data which could be used to develop teamload measurement but this usually needs adaptation to the particular setting and needs of the team.

Aggregating individual caseloads can be used as a beginning of a teamload system but it needs to be adapted to include **all the work of the team**. There may be reasons why teams do not want to know about their total workload. Sometimes team members are carrying hidden work which is regarded as 'not strictly necessary' by senior staff, or staff may be 'over' or 'under' in their work/caseloads.

In any teamload system there needs to be some form of weighting to allow for the hidden effort of risk and decision making involved in the team's work. Direct work with service users and working across complex systems, whether professional or social, should be included in any teamload monitoring process.

A teamload system allows teams to see the 'big numbers' and plan a collective team response. It helps locate where some short term team work is appropriate and allows a wider repertoire than individual case allocation, for example a series of visits to the duty team by parents with difficult adolescents may result in a support group rather than individual allocation.

Teamload management helps to locate trends in the work coming forward, particularly if it does not fit a departmental case category. It should require a department or a team to reconsider their activities against underlying principles and be aware of the various ways work is presented. For example a family problem could be presented as:

- drug using parents **or**
- child care issues in a community care assessment **or**
- a child in need where there is domestic violence.

All three are valid presentations of difficulties in the same family.

Exercise 9

For discussion in a team meeting:

- Is there a caseload management system in place? Is there a teamload management system in operation for your team? If not, how do you as a team communicate the input and output of your team?
- Are there systems in place in other parts of the organisation which you could adapt for your own use?
- Can teamload management systems build on caseload monitoring systems already in use in your organisation?
- What would you and your team like to know more about? What do you want to measure?

Section 7
Knowledge based practice

This section outlines a definition of knowledge based practice and some of the resulting issues and questions about the concept. Use the following as a starter for a team discussion about knowledge based practice.

Knowledge based practice includes evidence or knowledge from a variety of sources. Knowledge based practice developed from the concept of evidence based practice, which itself grew from the increasing drive for more effective decision making in social work throughout the 1980s and continues in the 1990s.

Knowledge based practice draws upon evidence from:

- custom and practice
- research findings
- policy guidance and the aims and objectives of the organisation
- the service user's views, needs and wishes
- resource availability
- locality or neighbourhood resources
- the law
- practice wisdom
- values, ethics and principles of social work.

Knowledge based practice is therefore not randomly controlled research evidence. It is making the best informed decisions and judgements using a whole range of information. It is also intended to respect the skills, expertise and values which underpin day to day practice and to give more prominence to the views of service users.

Knowledge based practice goes beyond the managerial approach to ensuring quality in social work. However, as most social work decisions are made within a bureaucratic organisation, this context has to be taken into account. How practitioners and social work managers learn and develop their knowledge base and apply it in practice is still a random and rather rocky road, with chance often playing too large a part in decision making.

Exercise 10

Think of a recent major decision taken with a family or client:

- What kind of knowledge informed this decision making process?
- Were there gaps in your knowledge base?
- What sources of knowledge did you use?

Exercise 11

- What systems are in place in your organisation to keep you up to date with innovations in social work practice or with research findings?
- How could they be improved?
- What responsibility do you think you have for keeping up to date?
- How could you improve on this?

Useful References

Brown, J. (1996) *Chance Favours the Prepared Mind*. London: HMSO

Harding, T. and Beresford, P. (1996) *The Standards We Expect*. London: NISW

Hughes, L. and Pengelly, P. (1997) *Supervision in Turbulent Times*. London: Jessica Kingsley

Le Riche, P.and Tanner, K. (1998) *Observation and its Application to Social Work*. London: Jessica Kingsley

McCaughan, N. and Palmer, B. (1994) *Systems Thinking for Harassed Managers*. London: Karnac

Menzies-Lyth, I. (1998) *Containing Anxiety in Institutions*. Selected Essays Vol. 1. London: Free Association

Morrision, T. (1994) *Staff Supervision in Social Care: An Action Learning Approach*. Harlow: Longman

Obholzer, A. and Roberts,V.Z. (1994) *The Unconscious at Work*. London: Routledge

Smale G. (1998) *Managing Change Through Innovation*. London: The Stationary Office

Smale, G. (1996) *Mapping Change and Innovation*. London: HMSO

Smale, G. and Tuson, G. with Biehal, N. and Marsh, P. (1993) *Empowerment, Assessment, Care Management and the Skilled Worker*. London: HMSO